© Aladdin Books Ltd 1990

*First published in
the United States in 1990 by*
Gloucester Press
387 Park Avenue South
New York NY 10016

Printed in Belgium

The publishers would like to acknowledge that
the photographs reproduced within this book
have been posed by models or have been
obtained from photographic agencies.

Design	David West
	Children's Book Design
Editor	Elise Bradbury
Picture Research	Cecilia Weston-Baker
Illustrator	Banjo Illustration

*The author, Dr. John Becklake, is Head of the
Department of Engineering, Science Museum,
London. The book is written in collaboration with
Sue Becklake.*

*The consultant, Brian Gardiner, is an atmospheric
scientist. He works for the British Antarctic Survey
and was one of the three scientists who discovered
the hole in the ozone layer.*

Library of Congress Cataloging-in-Publication Data

Becklake, John.
    Pollution / John Becklake.
      p. cm. -- (Green issues)
    Summary: Examines the problems of both industrial and domestic
pollution, their effects on the environment, the issues of international
control and responsibility, and the long-term hazards.
    ISBN 0-531-17233-3
    1. Pollution-- Juvenile literature. 2. Air-Pollution--Juvenile literature. [1.
Pollution.] I. Title. II. Series.
TD176.B43   1990
363.73--dc20   90-3218 CIP   AC

POLLUTION

JOHN AND SUE BECKLAKE

GLOUCESTER PRESS
London · New York · Toronto · Sydney

CONTENTS

▷ Pollution pours into the air from ordinary
houses with coal fires as well as from industrial
plants like this one producing "smokeless" fuel.

Introduction

Every few years we are all shocked by reports of pollution disasters. In 1984 toxic gas from a chemical plant killed thousands of people at Bhopal in India. Then in 1986 an accident at the Chernobyl nuclear reactor in the Soviet Union produced a radioactive cloud, which spread over much of Europe and Scandinavia. In 1989 the *Exxon Valdez* oil tanker ran aground and fouled many of Alaska's beaches with oil, killing birds, fish and other animals. These events hit the headlines, but less dramatic pollution is causing increasing problems all around us. Garbage, sewage and factory wastes have killed fish in many lakes and rivers and have polluted drinking water supplies. The air over many large cities can become a health risk when sunlight turns the gases that pour from car exhausts into noxious smog. The soil near some factory sites or waste dumps contains dangerous amounts of heavy metals or other poisonous materials.

These problems occur mainly in the industrialized countries, but they are beginning to spread worldwide. Carbon dioxide gas is building up in the atmosphere and threatening to change the climate of the world. Acid rain is damaging lakes and forests, and CFC gases from refrigerators and spray cans are destroying the ozone layer. In all these cases, the effects of pollution are felt a long way from its source.

The developed countries produce most of these pollutants with large-scale industry, extravagant use of energy, and dependence on automobiles, but the whole world is suffering. We are seriously damaging our planet with pollution, and since we rely on the earth and its atmosphere for our survival, we are only storing up trouble for the future. It is not too late to halt this destruction, but we will have to act fast and work together to stop the increase of pollution and control its effects.

CHAPTER ONE

WHAT IS POLLUTION?

It is not easy to define pollution. A dictionary defines it as "the contamination of one substance by another so that the former is unfit for its intended use." Substances that are useful or even essential in certain places at certain quantities can become pollutants if they occur in too large a quantity or in the wrong place. Artificial fertilizers enable farmers to grow more crops, but they can also seep from the soil to pollute our water supplies. Pollution takes many different forms: noise, radio waves and even heat, the more obvious types like solid litter, fumes from car exhausts, liquids from chemical factories and nuclear radiation. However, we can be sure that the problems caused by pollution are serious and increasingly threaten to poison the whole of the earth.

△ A rapidly growing population means more pollution everywhere, such as here in Athens.

Pollution all around us

Perhaps the most obvious kind of pollution is garbage and litter. Domestic trash consists of the material we throw away because we no longer need it: plastic bags, old cans, rusty bicycles and so on. It is a nuisance when people dump it on the streets, but it is probably one of the least harmful kinds of pollution. It is just one of many different types of land, water and air pollution, which are often interlinked.

Sulfur dioxide and nitrogen oxide gases, released into the air by power stations and industry, cause the acid rain which falls to earth, polluting the water in lakes and rivers. Water also picks up pollutants from land. When nuclear radiation escapes into the environment it pollutes land, air and water. It is difficult to isolate pollution problems; they have to be looked at as a whole. Air and water pass freely across borders between countries, so much pollution travels around the world. This means the problem must be tackled by international cooperation.

△ The air over major cities like New York is often clouded with pollution from factories and cars.

Natural cycles

Left to itself, nature has not changed significantly through human history because most natural processes occur in cycles. Water evaporates from the oceans, forming clouds, and then falls back to earth as rain when the clouds blow over the land, eventually returning to the sea via streams, lakes, and rivers. When living things die they decay, are broken down by organisms and bacteria to become nutrients in the soil for growing plants, which may, in turn, provide food for animals and humans.

Nothing is wasted and nature produces relatively little pollution. The gases we use from the air are recycled. Animals breathe in oxygen and release carbon dioxide, while plants use up carbon dioxide and release oxygen during photosynthesis. So the gases in the air remain essentially in balance when left to nature.

Human activity has disturbed these natural cycles. In the last one hundred years we have learned to make new materials, turning oil and coal into plastics, pesticides, fertilizers and thousands of other useful materials. The problem is that these materials often do not fit in with the natural cycles. There are no bacteria or other naturally-occurring agents to break them back down into the substances they were made from. Once produced, they stay as they are even when we have finished with them. Thus, plastic packaging piles up on trash heaps, and pesticides get into our food and drinking water.

Air pollution

The air that keeps us alive by supplying us with oxygen to breathe is really a mixture of gases: nitrogen, oxygen, carbon dioxide and several inert gases. The air surrounding the earth is in a thin layer called the atmosphere. This mixture has evolved gradually but since the evolution of humans, the atmosphere has remained more or less as we know it today.

Now our activities threaten to change this balance. It is not the two main gases in the atmosphere, nitrogen and oxygen, that are

5

affected, but others that occur in much smaller quantities. The amount of carbon dioxide in the atmosphere has been growing steadily for the past two hundred years with the growth of industry, and more recently, the dramatic increase in the number of cars.

This is a worldwide problem because carbon dioxide is a greenhouse gas, meaning it helps to trap heat in the atmosphere, keeping the planet warm. However, too much carbon dioxide traps too much heat and threatens to cause world climate changes. Another problem is the destruction of the ozone layer. This layer of gas high up in the atmosphere protects all living things from dangerous ultraviolet radiation from the Sun. It is now being destroyed by gases made by humans. Air pollution is often "exported" from one country to another, like acid rain which kills trees and damages lakes in many countries, especially in Europe and North America. Other pollution effects, like the smogs that form over some major cities, are local so they are probably easier to tackle. All humans and animals breathe air into the delicate tissues of the lungs, so it is vital to health to keep this air as free from damaging pollutants as possible.

Water pollution

Over two-thirds of the earth is covered with water, and life could not exist without it. We need water to drink as well as for crop irrigation. Industry uses vast quantities for cleaning, cooling and for many other industrial processes.

Our rivers, lakes and oceans teem with a myriad of life forms – plants, fish and animals – ranging in size from microscopic organisms to gigantic whales, many providing important sources of food. We rely on fairly clean water for most uses, but clean does not mean absolutely pure. All natural water contains many impurities like minerals or decaying matter, but these are

parts of natural cycles so they do not become pollutants in small quantities.

However, humans are now adding more waste materials like sewage, industrial effluent and garbage to our natural water resources. Sewage in reasonable quantities breaks down naturally, but we are now pouring it into seas and lakes in such vast amounts that nature cannot cope with it. Oil from tanker disasters can devastate coastal areas. Nitrates and phosphates from fertilizers, sewage and cleaning materials get into the water where they cause rapid growth of vegetation. When it dies and decomposes, this vegetation uses up the oxygen in the water, so fish and other aquatic life can no longer survive there. Polluted water can support few living things, can only be drunk after extensive purification, and is not even safe to swim in.

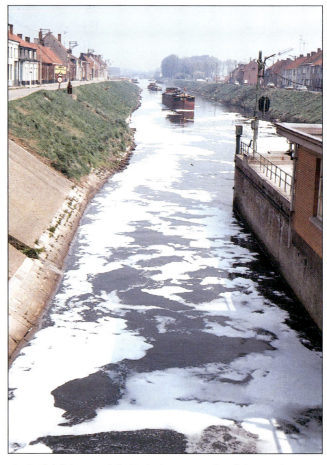

△ Rubbish on this Belgian canal adds to the unseen pollution in the water.

△ Nuclear accidents can contaminate grass with radiation, making cow's milk dangerous.

Land pollution

Like the air and water, land is polluted from many different sources. Some pollution is unsightly, like trash dropped at a picnic site or during a major event like a football game, but probably the worst land pollution problems are caused by the disposal of industrial waste. This waste is often toxic or hazardous and is frequently dumped in holes in the ground, like old quarries or mines, from which it can slowly seep into the surrounding soil and eventually into the water supply. Although it may originally be sealed in containers, the waste may outlive the container, and escape to pollute the environment.

Nuclear radiation is not just a local pollutant. Radioactive fallout released into the atmosphere from nuclear disasters like Chernobyl and from nuclear weapons testing can affect vast areas of land and remain dangerous long after the event.

Heavy metals like cadmium, sometimes found in the soil near industrial sites, and lead from car exhausts, are taken up by food crops grown in contaminated soil, making them unsafe to eat. Some pesticides, particularly DDT which is now banned in many countries, though not worldwide, persist in the soil for years and accumulate in the food chain reaching concentrations that are toxic to many living things.

Space and sound

While despoiling the planet we live on, humans are also spreading litter into outer space. Orbiting around the Earth are many operating satellites. Among these are old, no longer functioning satellites, parts of rockets, and other space litter. Near the earth these fall back into the atmosphere in a few years and break apart harmlessly, but deeper in space, objects may stay in orbit for thousands of years.

Noise can also be regarded as pollution, especially if you live near a large airport or building site, or are troubled by neighbors who like to play loud music. Persistent loud noise from pneumatic drills or even discos can severely damage your hearing if you do not protect your ears. These days the air is buzzing with radio signals carrying television, radio and huge quantities of information. There are strict controls to minimize interference, but there is still pollution from overcrowded frequencies and illegal radio stations (pirate radio). There are also reports that electromagnetic waves may be a real pollutant, possibly endangering human health.

△ Humans have even polluted the Moon with space probes, including Apollo landing craft.

CHAPTER TWO

THE CAUSES OF POLLUTION

Where does pollution come from? Each of us produces small amounts of garbage and sewage each day. This becomes significant when it is multiplied by the number of people in the world, which is increasing all the time. However, the main contributors to the problems of pollution are the electrical power stations and the industries that make the huge variety of goods we use all the time. Other major culprits are means of transportation, particularly cars, because of the huge numbers of them, and modern intensive farming. In fact, humans do very little without producing pollution, and most of it is produced in the rich, industrialized countries in the northern hemisphere of the world.

Natural pollution

We usually assume that all pollution is made by people. However, if we define pollution as materials in places where they would not normally occur, and in too large a quantity to be easily absorbed or recycled, then natural kinds of pollution do exist. These include volcanic eruptions, forest fires and even large meteorites from outer space. Meteorites very rarely hit the earth, but in the very distant past their effects were catastrophic. Some scientists think that the dinosaurs became extinct as a result of a massive meteorite hitting the earth and drastically changing the world's climate. Forest fires, which can start naturally, pollute the atmosphere with smoke and carbon dioxide from burning wood.

△ Oil refineries pollute the air with gases which add to the greenhouse effect either by releasing methane gas, or by burning it and releasing carbon dioxide.

◁ Every year there are 20 to 30 volcanic eruptions around the world which produce ash, lava and gases. Thus, humans are not responsible for all pollution.

Volcanoes pollute both the atmosphere and the land. Their ash and lava flows can devastate the surrounding countryside and they can spew out enormous clouds of dust and gas. Some of the dust falls locally, but some also rises into the upper atmosphere and is carried right around the world, sometimes causing a cooling of the climate which can last for years. In 1963, the dust and gas cloud from the eruption of the Agung volcano in Indonesia rose high into the stratosphere. The gases emitted from volcanoes include carbon monoxide, carbon dioxide, hydrogen sulfide and sulfur dioxide, all of which are air pollutants also produced by modern industrial processes.

The generation of electricity

In the industrial countries of the world electricity has become essential to our way of life. Electricity supplies heating, lighting and cooking for most of us, and powers our washing machines, refrigerators, televisions, stereos and computers. It also supplies business and industry with most of its power.

Electricity is often advertised as "clean" power, but although it may be clean to use, the power stations that generate electricity produce a great deal of air pollution. About 75 percent of our electricity is made by burning fossil fuels (coal, oil and gas). When fossil fuels burn they release gases including carbon dioxide, sulfur dioxide, and oxides of nitrogen, all of which pollute the atmosphere. Carbon dioxide is the main gas causing the greenhouse effect, which threatens to change the world climate. Sulfur dioxide and nitrogen oxides cause acid rain and also contribute to smog.

Burning oil produces more pollution than burning natural gas, but burning coal is the most damaging. A typical coal-burning power station producing 2,000 megawatts of electricity, enough to supply a city of about two million people, burns seven million tons of coal a year and releases 20 million tons of carbon dioxide, 150 thousand tons of sulfur dioxide and 50 thousand tons of nitrogen oxides each year.

However, not all electricity comes from power stations burning coal, oil or gas; nuclear power is another contributor to our energy supply. Nuclear energy does not pollute the atmosphere with carbon dioxide and sulfur dioxide, but it has other problems, such as radioactive pollution. Nuclear power was originally expected to be a clean, cheap source of electricity, but has become very unpopular because many people fear the risk of a radioactive leak or worse, an accidental explosion.

One of the biggest problems of nuclear power is what to do with the radioactive waste. Used fuel rods from nuclear power stations are extremely radioactive and will remain lethal for thousands of years. This waste must be prevented from polluting the environment. Perhaps one solution is to look at other ways we can produce electricity without harming the environment, for instance by increasing our use of clean, renewable resources, such as solar, wind and water power.

Industrial effluent
Industry supplies us with most of the things we use at home, work and school, including luxuries like televisions, as well as more essential things like medicines and processed food products. But industry also has a range of harmful effects on the environment, including the fact that many factories and industrial plants are extremely unsightly, causing what is often called visual pollution. Also, like power stations, many industries burn fossil fuels for heat and power, adding to air pollution.

However, the worst problem they cause is the bewildering array of waste materials, solid, liquid and gas, left from industrial processes. Some are relatively harmless; paper mills and textile factories use water in large quantities and pump it back into rivers where, although it is not dangerous, the impurities from the factory all add to water pollution. However, a great deal of industrial waste is much more dangerous, and this hazardous waste must be disposed of very carefully to avoid poisoning people and the environment. There are many different kinds of hazardous waste, mainly produced by the electronics, chemical, petroleum and plastics industries. Worldwide, more than 400 million tons of hazardous waste is produced each year, about 90 percent of this is from the industrialized countries.

It is not only the waste that is dangerous, but also some of the products. One example of an extremely dangerous product is the PCBs (polychlorinated biphenyls) which were used extensively in the electrical industry until their dangers were discovered. Now they are banned in many countries except in sealed equipment. When they are no longer needed they can be burned in special incinerators, but if the temperature is not carefully controlled, even more dangerous materials can be produced. There are not many suitable waste disposal facilities so these dangerous chemicals often have to be shipped around the world before they can be disposed of safely. Many other toxic wastes are destroyed by burning, but some of the less dangerous materials are buried in holes in the ground, called landfill sites. Sometimes they are sealed in containers, which may corrode and leak, and some waste is pumped underground. These methods are not very satisfactory even when used responsibly, and chemicals have been known to leak from landfill sites into the surrounding area.

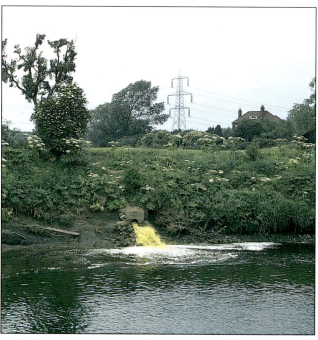
△ Polluted water is often pumped into rivers.

△ Pesticides sprayed onto crops may blow onto the surrounding countryside.

Agriculture – pollution or food?

The world's farms pollute the air, land and water. They release nitrogen oxides and methane gases into the air from paddy fields, plants and animals. They also produce smoke when straw and stubble are burned in the fields after harvest. When large numbers of animals are kept indoors and their wastes are allowed to accumulate in slurry pits, these get too concentrated to use as manure and become a pollution problem instead of a natural fertilizer.

However, the main problems stem from the increasing use of artificial fertilizers and pesticides. Their use has been necessary because the population of the world has been growing dramatically, especially over the last 50 years. Each year there are about 80 to 90 million people to feed, and farms have had to provide the extra food needed from about the same amount of land.

Before World War II, farms used to grow a variety of crops and kept a range of different animals. The animal wastes were returned to the land as manure which slowly broke down in the soil, providing nutrients for the growing crops and keeping the soil in good condition. Now, on modern intensive farms, manufactured fertilizers are used to supplement or even replace

manure. Although modern fertilizers supply the substances the plants need for strong healthy growth, they do not keep the soil in good condition. The rain washes them out of the soil where they are needed, into rivers and underground water reserves where they become pollutants.

Pesticides are used to kill the pests and diseases which destroy or spoil crops during growth or while in storage. There are three main types of pesticide: insecticides which kill insects; herbicides which kill weeds, and fungicides which stop fungus diseases. These chemicals must be used carefully because they are essentially poisons and become serious pollutants when they get into the water supply or onto food.

Many insecticides kill all insects indiscriminately, including the beneficial ones, like bees which are needed for pollination, and predatory insects that eat harmful insects, keeping them under control naturally. Another problem is that insects can become resistant to some insecticides, making the chemicals ineffective unless used in increasingly stronger concentrations. DDT and dieldrin are two insecticides that have been banned or restricted in many countries because they are so dangerous.

11

Transportation

All types of transportation produce pollution, mainly by emitting gases into the air. Most means of transportation rely on fossil fuels (usually oil) for power, burning gasoline or diesel fuel. Even electric trains get their power originally from the fossil fuels which were burned to supply the electricity. When burned, fossil fuels release carbon dioxide, sulfur dioxide and nitrogen oxide gases. Car exhausts produce poisonous carbon monoxide gas, droplets of unburned fuel and, in some cases, lead. It is also estimated that every year the average American car releases its own weight of carbon into the air as gas. However, the use of lead-free gasoline in the United States has helped to reduce auto emissions. The mixture of gases from car exhausts reacts with sunlight, making the bad-smelling, unhealthy smog which hangs over many large cities. Smog contains the poisonous gas, ozone, which damages plants and causes eye irritation when it pollutes the atmosphere at ground level. However, ozone is not a pollutant high in the upper atmosphere, where it protects life on earth from the Sun's dangerous ultraviolet radiation.

Individual aircraft and rockets also produce pollutants and in much larger quantities, but since there are fewer of them the problems they cause are not as severe. Yet they do deliver their pollutants high in the atmosphere where they may damage the ozone layer.

Ships pollute the sea. Dangerous cargoes are sometimes lost overboard if a ship is wrecked. The most frequent pollution by ships at sea is oil, occasionally from disastrous shipwrecks, but sometimes from deliberate dumping when washing out tanks, though this is now illegal. For every thousand tons of oil extracted from underground, roughly one ton finds its way into the oceans as pollution.

△ Car exhausts pollute the air in Mexico City.

Pollution from the home

A modern household is the cause of much pollution. A typical suburban home in an industrialized country uses about 8,000 kilowatt hours of electricity in a year. To produce this amount, about three tons of coal will have been burned at a power station, releasing about ten tons of carbon dioxide into the atmosphere. This does not include heating, which also uses up fossil fuels in the form of coal, oil or gas. Most families run at least one car which burns gasoline. All these add to air pollution.

Then there is household garbage which will go to make up land pollution. Down the sink goes dirty water, with soap, detergents and many other materials, which are joined by the toilets' contents on the way to the sewage works. Not all of this dirty water is cleaned up by sewage

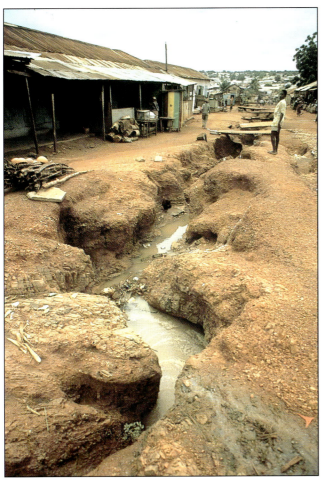
△ Sewage spreads diseases in poor areas.

rapidly increasing world population, but this is not the only reason. In the industrialized parts of the world, each one of us has used more energy, we have produced more cars, and we have used artificial fertilizers and pesticides at an ever-increasing rate. Gradually, materials made by humans have proliferated, along with their potential to cause pollution by not decaying easily. Plastics have largely replaced paper for packaging, and artificial fibers are increasingly used in clothing and other fabrics. Since the 1950s farmers have come to rely on artificial pesticides and fertilizers. Scientists have recorded the increase of carbon dioxide in the atmosphere and we have become more aware of pollution all around us.

However, it is not all bad news. When the price of oil rose in the oil crisis of the 1970s, we discovered how to be economical with energy. Oil consumption dropped, lessening the pollution released when oil is burned. More recently, acid rain damage in Europe, the discovery of a "hole" in the ozone layer, and warnings of global warming have led to reductions in the output of sulfur dioxide, and carbon dioxide in some countries. In 1989, major industrialized nations agreed to ban production of CFCs by the end of the century.

treatment plants. Some is only partially treated, and some not cleaned at all before being pumped into the sea. In developing countries the situation is worse: only eight of India's towns and cities fully treat sewage, while many others return raw sewage to rivers whose water is used downstream for bathing and drinking.

In the house the aerosol-spray cans of deodorant, polish, and air freshener, among other things, may still contain CFCs which damage the ozone layer, though these are being phased out. Yet CFCs remain in refrigerators and freezers. Our fight against pollution must start in our homes.

Is it getting worse? Or better?
Since the turn of the century, the amount of pollution we have created has greatly increased. This is sometimes blamed on the

Exporting pollution
Pesticides, such as DDT, which are banned in their country of origin, are still exported to developing countries where rural workers do not know of their dangers. This can affect countries importing food contaminated with pesticides. Some unscrupulous companies dump their toxic waste in developing countries where inadequate controls may result in serious pollution.

13

Pollution and health

We cannot escape the pollution around us. In cities, polluted air results in smog which hurts lungs and eyes. Industry and its waste dumps spread poisonous materials in the soil and eventually the water supply, causing an increase in the number of cancer cases. Severe industrial pollution actually shortens average lifetimes. Pollution can be even more dangerous in poorer countries which cannot afford the controls necessary for the safe use of dangerous chemicals. Some 75 percent of all deaths from pesticide poisoning happen in developing countries, though they use only 15 percent of the world's pesticides. Untreated, polluted water also endangers the health and even the lives of millions of people all over the world.

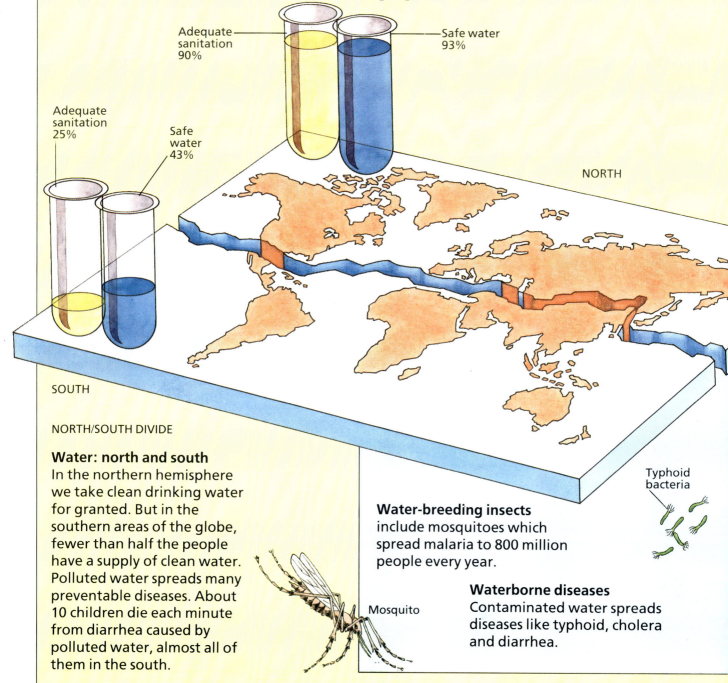

Adequate sanitation 90%

Safe water 93%

Adequate sanitation 25%

Safe water 43%

NORTH

SOUTH

NORTH/SOUTH DIVIDE

Typhoid bacteria

Mosquito

Water: north and south
In the northern hemisphere we take clean drinking water for granted. But in the southern areas of the globe, fewer than half the people have a supply of clean water. Polluted water spreads many preventable diseases. About 10 children die each minute from diarrhea caused by polluted water, almost all of them in the south.

Water-breeding insects
include mosquitoes which spread malaria to 800 million people every year.

Waterborne diseases
Contaminated water spreads diseases like typhoid, cholera and diarrhea.

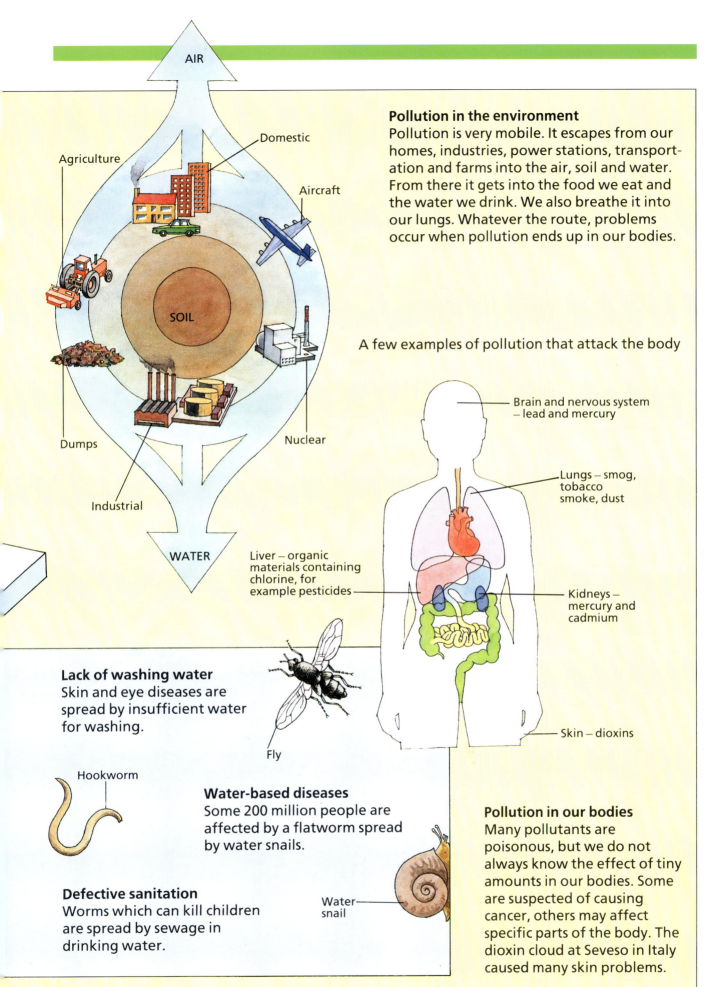

AIR

Agriculture

Domestic

Aircraft

SOIL

Dumps

Nuclear

Industrial

WATER

Pollution in the environment

Pollution is very mobile. It escapes from our homes, industries, power stations, transportation and farms into the air, soil and water. From there it gets into the food we eat and the water we drink. We also breathe it into our lungs. Whatever the route, problems occur when pollution ends up in our bodies.

A few examples of pollution that attack the body

Brain and nervous system – lead and mercury

Lungs – smog, tobacco smoke, dust

Liver – organic materials containing chlorine, for example pesticides

Kidneys – mercury and cadmium

Skin – dioxins

Lack of washing water
Skin and eye diseases are spread by insufficient water for washing.

Fly

Hookworm

Water-based diseases
Some 200 million people are affected by a flatworm spread by water snails.

Pollution in our bodies
Many pollutants are poisonous, but we do not always know the effect of tiny amounts in our bodies. Some are suspected of causing cancer, others may affect specific parts of the body. The dioxin cloud at Seveso in Italy caused many skin problems.

Defective sanitation
Worms which can kill children are spread by sewage in drinking water.

Water snail

CHAPTER THREE

THE EFFECTS OF POLLUTION

Pollution is beginning to have a growing impact on all our lives. Some problems affect the whole world, such as potential global warming due to the increasing greenhouse effect, and damage to the ozone layer, which allows more ultraviolet radiation to reach the earth. Other pollution problems are more localized, though acid rain travels hundreds of miles killing trees and damaging lakes in other countries. Pollution of the air, water and soil throughout the industrialized countries poses a threat to our health in general, and reduces life expectancy where pollution is allowed to pour into the environment unchecked.

Overheating greenhouse

For nearly one hundred years scientists have warned that the increasing amount of carbon dioxide in the atmosphere could cause problems. Although there is relatively little carbon dioxide there, it is a very important part of the atmosphere. With oxygen it forms a cycle that allows organisms to breathe and plants to manufacture food. Carbon dioxide also insulates the earth, keeping it warm by trapping the heat produced by the Sun. Without this natural greenhouse effect the earth would on average be about 86°F cooler than it is now.

However, since around the year 1800 we have been adding more and more carbon dioxide to the atmosphere as a pollutant, mostly by burning fossil fuels. At first it was coal; then oil was also used; and now we burn coal, oil and gas in our homes, industries and power stations, as well as gasoline and diesel in cars and trucks. Some carbon dioxide is also produced when

◁ Burning the rainforests adds to the greenhouse effect by releasing carbon dioxide into the air. Then if the land is used for grazing cattle, they will produce another greenhouse gas, methane, during their digestive process.

◁ Children wait for food relief from abroad when the harvest fails because of lack of rain. We do not know if the increasing greenhouse effect will make the semidesert regions better or worse food-producing areas.

rainforests are burned to clear the land for farming. Not only does the burning wood give off carbon dioxide, but the trees whose leaves normally absorb carbon dioxide are destroyed altogether. The level of carbon dioxide in the air was steady until a few centuries ago, but since then it has increased by about 30 percent. As long as we continue to burn fossil fuels, the level of carbon dioxide will continue to increase.

Carbon dioxide is not the only "greenhouse gas." Other gases trap the Sun's heat even better, including methane, nitrous oxide and CFCs. Nitrous oxide comes from decaying organic material, and methane is found in natural gas fields and is produced by paddy fields, rotting garbage and even cows' stomachs. CFCs, on the other hand, are manufactured gases which have ill effects. Although there are only tiny quantities of these polluting gases, they are gradually building up in the atmosphere, damaging the ozone layer and trapping heat.

No one really knows specifically what the effects of the increase of these gases in the atmosphere will be, but scientists expect the average temperature of the earth will rise by about 9 to 18°F if the carbon dioxide level of doubles. It is believed that this will change the climate around the world, making the overall weather hotter, but cloudier and wetter. However, some fertile crop-growing areas may get drier while other desert areas could become more fertile, possibly changing the balance of economic power for some countries.

The ice caps would melt, the water in the oceans would increase, raising sea levels which have already risen six inches since 1880. The sea level could be another 12 inches higher by 2030 – flooding homes and farmland in some low-lying coastal areas. Scientists do not know for certain if this process, called global warming, has started yet, and by the time they are able to prove their fears, even more greenhouse gases will be polluting the earth's atmosphere.

Destroying the ozone layer

Some effects of pollution take us by surprise. This happened in 1984 when scientists were measuring the ozone high in the atmosphere over the Antarctic. They found that during the Antarctic spring about one third of the ozone disappeared, but most of it reappeared in the summer.

The ozone layer exists high in the atmosphere where ozone and oxygen are constantly interchanging. It absorbs ultraviolet radiation from the Sun and protects the earth from the damaging effects of this radiation which would kill plant life and cause harmful effects in humans, including severe sunburn, skin cancer and cataracts of the eyes. Scientists discovered that CFC gases were destroying ozone in the special conditions over the Antarctic at the end of the winter months. CFCs are manufactured gases that have many uses because they are not poisonous and they are long-lived and stable. They are used to eject the contents of spray cans, and are used in refrigerators, air-conditioners and in the manufacture of polyurethane foam.

Because they last for about 100 years, CFCs survive to filter through to the upper atmosphere, where extremely tiny amounts can do enormous damage. Scientists had been worried about the effects on the ozone layer from the exhausts of high-flying aircraft or rockets as well as CFCs, but they had not expected the sudden, dramatic effect measured over the Antarctic. In 1987 and 1989 the spring reduction in the ozone was over 50 percent and the ozone was reduced over inhabited areas of New Zealand and Australia for the first time. There has also been a small reduction in the ozone layer over the rest of the earth. However, even if we stop using all CFC gases now, the damage will probably continue for a hundred years.

Acid rain

The previous two cases of pollution affect the atmosphere worldwide. Acid rain is more localized, but can still cross international boundaries and affect wide

areas. Its most severe effects have occurred in Europe but it is now affecting places as far apart as North America and Australia. Normal rain is slightly acidic, but some pollutants make it much more acidic, sometimes as strong as vinegar. These pollutants are the sulfur dioxide and nitrogen oxides that pour out of most coal-burning power station chimneys and car exhausts. They mix with moisture in the air making weak solutions of sulfuric and nitric acids that are carried in clouds by the wind until they fall as rain – often in other countries. Power station chimneys are built very tall in order to stop the pollutants from falling nearby, but this means the discharges travel farther before returning to earth. Acid rain caused by British power stations falls on Scandinavia and northern

Europe, and pollution created by the United States falls as acid rain on Canada. It is estimated that 90 percent of the acid rain falling on Norway originates in other countries. Around the world about one half of the sulfur in the air comes from natural sources like sea spray, rotting vegetation and plankton. However, in Europe only 15 percent is natural. The other 85 percent is created by humans. Between 50 and 75 million tons of sulfur are poured into the air each year.

Acid rain is having a devastating effect on the rivers, lakes and forests where it falls. It makes the water in the rivers and lakes acidic, washes nutrients out of the soil and releases aluminum from the soil into the lakes. The combination of acid and aluminum in the water kills the fish that live there, leaving lakes with crystal-clear water lined with algae and moss, which reduce the variety of life in the water even further. In Sweden 60,00 miles of rivers and streams are affected, and 18,000 lakes are damaged, 4,500 so badly that they have no fish in them. Forest trees are starved of nutrients and poisoned by the aluminum so they lose their leaves and eventually die. Over half the trees in Germany, Holland, Britain, Switzerland and Czechoslovakia are said to be damaged and about 16 percent of the fir and pine forests in Germany are dead.

In New York's Adirondack Region, 25 percent of the lakes and ponds are so acidic that they cannot support fish, and another 20 percent are seriously affected. Massachusetts and Pennsylvania also report serious acid rain effects on their lakes and rivers – and despite attempts at pollution control, these effects are spreading.

◁ Damage to trees in forests far from industrial towns was first reported in the 1970s. Now acid rain has affected almost half the trees in Germany and about a fourth have actually died, like these in the Black Forest.

△ Protesters try to stop raw sewage being dumped into the sea.

Dead rivers and dying seas

It is not only acid rain that pollutes rivers and streams. All through history people have used flowing rivers to carry their waste away from their towns and villages. While the population was small and the waste was mostly sewage this caused no problems. In small amounts sewage is easily absorbed by rivers and seas and breaks down naturally into harmless materials. However, our rapidly increasing population produces too much waste to be absorbed easily, and sewage is now mixed with chemicals from detergents and cleaning liquids. Sewage and other vegetable matter provide a rich source of food for bacteria and microorganisms living in the water, and these flourish along with tiny water plants called algae. These all use up the oxygen dissolved in the water, and without oxygen fish suffocate and die. Nitrates from artificial fertilizers and phosphates from detergents and cleaning fluids also stimulate plant growth. This blocks rivers and uses up oxygen when the plants die and decay, leaving stretches of waterway virtually lifeless and smelly. These problems travel down the rivers into lakes and seas which also suffer if they are enclosed, like North America's Great Lakes and the Mediterranean Sea.

Industry has also been allowed to add to the pollution in the rivers and seas. It was assumed that if the waste materials were not very poisonous or if they were released in very small quantities, they would disperse harmlessly in the water. However, some pollutants are concentrated in the food chain. Tiny aquatic organisms eat minute quantities of pollutants which are stored in their bodies. As the smaller creatures are eaten by larger ones, the concentration gradually builds up, sometimes becoming a million times more concentrated, and reaching poisonous levels for large fish or animals. This bioconcentration happened with the pesticide DDT in the 1950s and 1960s, reducing bird populations by making the shells of their eggs very thin. The dangers of DDT are now recognized, but other poisonous substances like PCBs, and the heavy metals cadmium and mercury, also persist and build up to dangerous levels in the food chains.

The North Sea is one of the most polluted seas on earth. It has algal blooms which scientists blame on untreated sewage, and badly polluted water still flows into it from the River Rhine in spite of attempts to clean it up. In addition, the countries bordering the North Sea use it as a dump for six million

△ Clean water is vital for good health.

tons of industrial waste, 6,000 tons of copper, 8,000 tons of lead and 900 tons of cadmium each year. Great Britain also dumps sewage sludge there and incinerator ships burn dangerous waste on its surface. As a result, the animal life is suffering. Pollution may also have contributed to the recent disease epidemics among seals and birds. Flat fish are also showing increased signs of cancer, ulcers and fin rot.

The most polluted island body of water in the United States is probably Onondaga Lake in New York. Mercury and other toxic chemicals were dumped there for many years, and clean-up efforts have so far been unsuccessful. The Guyahoga River, that caught fire in 1969 as a result of hot slag, oil and chemical dumping, is also an example of freshwater pollution – though here clean-up efforts have been slightly more successful.

Water – fit to drink?
We continue to dump garbage and sewage into rivers and then expect the same rivers to supply us with water clean enough to drink. In the developed countries we use enormous quantities of water, about 100 gallons per person per day in the United States for bathing, washing, and cooking as well as for drinking. The water from rivers like the Thames in Europe is removed, purified, used, and returned dirty to the river several times before it reaches the sea. In industrialized countries water is cleaned at purification plants before being piped to most homes. Dirty water and sewage are removed along main drains, usually via sewage works, before returning to the river or sea. Heavy metals, dangerous bacteria and organic waste are removed or killed, leaving the water relatively safe for us to drink.

However, chemicals like chlorine, which is itself a poison, are often used to sterilize our water and we do not know what problems this could cause in the future. Not all pollutants are removed by the purification process. In some areas the levels of nitrates from agriculture are higher than recommended, and traces of lead, aluminum and pesticides have also been found to pollute some drinking water. We tend to assume that water from deep wells and springs is clean and good to drink, but small amounts of pesticides and other pollutants enter those supplies as well. Because it can take many years for surface water to seep down through the soil to natural underground reservoirs, we can only expect water pollution to increase.

The situation is much worse in developing countries where very few homes have a piped supply of clean water or adequate sanitation. The luckier people have access to a well with relatively clean water, but in many cases water for all purposes is taken from the local river. The same river may already have had raw sewage dumped in it from other villages upstream. Thus many diseases like typhoid, cholera and yellow fever, which are spread by dirty water, cause at least 25 million deaths each year in developing countries, and almost none where a supply of clean water is taken for granted.

Hazardous waste

As soon as we throw something away at home or in industry it becomes potential pollution. Domestic trash is usually dumped, covered with soil and left to rot. As it decays it often generates methane gas, and it may contain small amounts of harmful chemicals. However, many industries produce hazardous wastes that are too dangerous to be released into waterways or dumped on ordinary landfills or dumps. Materials are said to be hazardous if, individually or in a mixture, they could be poisonous, corrosive, explosive, catch fire easily or react dangerously with water or other substances. They include heavy metals, pesticides like DDT, PCBs, and poisonous by-products of industrial processes, like dioxins.

These can be disposed of by dumping them in special landfill sites or in the deep ocean, or treated chemically or burned in incinerators. Although the last two methods are the safest, over 90 percent of the world's hazardous waste is still put into landfill sites. Some of these, called containment landfills, are lined with clay or plastic to prevent the waste from escaping indefinitely, but these can never be entirely leakproof and have been known to overflow. Others are just holes in the ground where the waste gradually seeps into the earth, theoretically to decompose naturally or become weak enough to be harmless. Eventually the water in the soil carries these poisons into rivers or underground water reserves and they turn up in our drinking water or food.

In some cases toxic wastes have contaminated whole areas. In the 1940s and 1950s a large chemical factory near Niagara Falls on the border of New York and Ontario, dumped over 20,000 tons of chemical waste in an abandoned canal called Love Canal. It was then covered with clay and earth, and a school and houses were built there. But more than the usual number of cancer cases and defects in babies born there began to emerge. In 1978 it was recognized as a serious health hazard and

△ Chemicals have poisoned Love Canal in the United States.

△ The Japanese company that polluted the sea with mercury at Minamata eventually paid compensation to the victims.

the whole area was permanently evacuated and declared a disaster area. By 1984, over 500 other landfill sites in the United States had been identified as hazardous to health.

Industries may also contaminate the local area around the plant. Heavy metals like lead and cadmium have been found in the soil and in food crops near iron and steel industries and metal smelting plants in particular. In one case in Japan the pollution from a zinc smelting factory was so severe that a whole village suffered from cadmium poisoning, which damages the kidneys and makes the bones very brittle.

Radiation and radioactive waste

Many people believe nuclear radiation is the most frightening kind of pollution because they understand so little about it. We do know that high levels of radiation cause severe illness and can kill people, while lower levels are linked with cancers, but we do not know if there is any safe lower limit. There are legal limits on radiation exposure for people working with radiation in the nuclear industry and medicine, and these limits are constantly being lowered as scientists learn more about the effects of low-level radiation.

However, we are also surrounded by various forms of natural radiation produced by rocks like granite, and from space as cosmic rays, and this accounts for most of the radiation people are exposed to. Medical sources like X rays provide additional exposure, while relatively little actually comes from nuclear power station wastes. Occasionally a nuclear accident or fallout from a nuclear explosion, though there are very few of these now, may add to these levels of exposure. However, we should not underestimate the serious problems of radioactive waste from the nuclear power stations which generated nearly 20 percent of the world's electricity in 1985.

A typical nuclear power station produces about 8 barrels of very dangerous, high-level radioactive waste every year. These and the medium-level wastes will remain dangerous for thousands of years. The only way to deal with them is to store them in tanks where they must be constantly cooled and stirred.

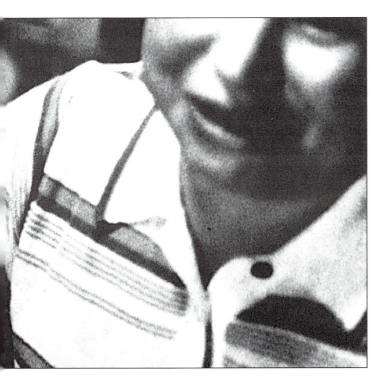

Minamata
In 1953 the people of the Japanese fishing village of Minamata began to suffer from nerve diseases including convulsions, blindness and brain damage. It was all caused by mercury poisoning. A nearby chemical plant making glue had discharged poisonous methyl mercury into the sea at Minamata Bay, contaminating the fish eaten by the local village people. By 1983 more than 300 people had died and about 1,500 more were still suffering from the effects.

In Britain this waste is stored in ever-increasing quantities at the Sellafield reprocessing plant. In the United States the storage tanks at the Hanford plant leaked about 530,000 gallons between 1945 and 1973, and radiation products were found in the groundwater, the Columbia River and the surrounding soil where levels of radioactive plutonium were 5,000 times above the permissible level.

The much less dangerous low-level waste is often buried, and until 1983 many drums of it were dumped in the oceans. Although this has now stopped, the fuel reprocessing site at Sellafield is still allowed to discharge low-level liquid waste right into the Irish Sea, which is now the most radioactive sea in the world. We will have to wait to see the long-term effects on people who eat fish caught in the Irish Sea. Already an abnormally high incidence of childhood leukemia, cancer of the blood cells, has occurred near nuclear power stations and research stations.

The most serious potential radiation hazard is probably from accidents at nuclear power plants. There have already been at least three serious accidents, at Windscale (now called Sellafield) in Britain in 1957, Three Mile Island in the United States in 1979, and Chernobyl in the Soviet Union in 1986, all releasing radiation into the environment. It is very difficult to make direct connections between these accidents and local health problems, apart from the immediate deaths from radiation sickness at Chernobyl. Nonetheless, the contamination of the land by radioactive fallout from Chernobyl is certain to give rise to many deaths from cancer for the next 50 years or more.

Pollution and our health

There are undoubtedly health hazards from radiation, but with this and the many other kinds of pollution it is not always easy to make a direct connection between a

△ Geiger counters were used to check people for radiation after the Chernobyl disaster.

particular form of pollution and damage to our health. Until very recently many people thought that the clusters of childhood leukemia cases near nuclear plants were caused by low-level radiation pollution, though this could not be proved. Now new research has indicated that the children of people working in the nuclear industry who are exposed to radiation doses near the legal limit may be more likely to suffer from leukemia, so the link is complicated. In other cases the effects are obvious, like the eye irritations and lung problems caused by smog. Then there is the self-inflicted pollution of cigarette smoke which causes lung and other cancers. We also know that lead from car exhausts gets into food crops grown near busy roads and ends up in our bodies, where it can damage the kidneys, brain and nervous system.

The results of exposure to high doses of some pollutants are revealed by disasters

△ Oil spills on beaches must be cleaned up carefully to avoid more damage to wildlife.

like the explosion at Seveso in Italy in 1976, where a cloud of dioxin was released and caused severe skin problems and increased birth defects among people living nearby. However, this does not tell us whether we should be worried by the tiny traces of poisonous substances in the air, water and soil. Various government authorities set limits for pollutants in food and water, but they often raise these limits if they are difficult to meet. This happened in Italy, where levels of pesticides in drinking water exceeded the "safe" limit. It also happened in Europe after the Chernobyl nuclear accident, where permitted radiation levels in food were raised in case of another nuclear accident!

In industrialized countries, cancers of all kinds are on the rise; about one American in three will have cancer during his or her lifetime and one in four will die of it. Cancer rates are particularly high in areas with a high concentration of chemical industries and hazardous waste dumps. In contrast, cancer is a rare disease in the developing world where there is comparatively little industry.

In some Eastern European countries industry has been allowed to operate with no thought at all for the effects of its pollution on the local people or the environment. As a result, in industrialized areas of Poland and Czechoslovakia, not only are pollution-related diseases much more common than elsewhere, but the life expectancy rate has actually fallen.

Getting away from pollution

We are not always aware of pollution, but we cannot get away from it, and its effects can make life unpleasant. Garbage dumps are unsightly, smelly and often support rats and other vermin. Nobody wants to live near one. Industrial slag heaps like those from coal mines scar the landscape and can be dangerous. In 1966, a slag heap at the Welsh mining village of Aberfan collapsed, burying a school and killing 116 children and 28 adults.

At the coast the sea may contain sewage which is unpleasant for swimmers and could spread diseases. The beaches themselves are often spoiled by litter or tar and oil which has washed ashore. Large oil spills ruin coastlines, wreaking havoc on the lives of the people in the area and killing birds, fish and animals indiscriminately. They are difficult to deal with because the detergent used to clean the beaches causes almost as much pollution as the oil itself. In cities we may be forced to breathe in the harmful gases in smogs, and it is not easy to escape from noise, which is irritating enough when it comes from appliances in our homes, but can be damaging at the higher levels found near large airports. What can we do to reduce the inconvenience and danger of all this pollution?

Pollution disasters

Disasters which dump huge quantities of pollution into the environment are almost always caused by human carelessness. Massive oil and chemical spills kill wildlife by the thousands, damage habitats and cost a great deal to clean up. Even worse are disasters which kill large numbers of people, and the long-term effects of some disasters like nuclear accidents are impossible to calculate.

Exxon Valdez 1989

The *Exxon Valdez* oil tanker hit rocks off Alaska spilling 11 million gallons of oil. It contaminated 1,180 miles of shore, the home of seals, otters, birds and fish. About 100,000 seabirds were probably killed and 36,000 were actually found dead.

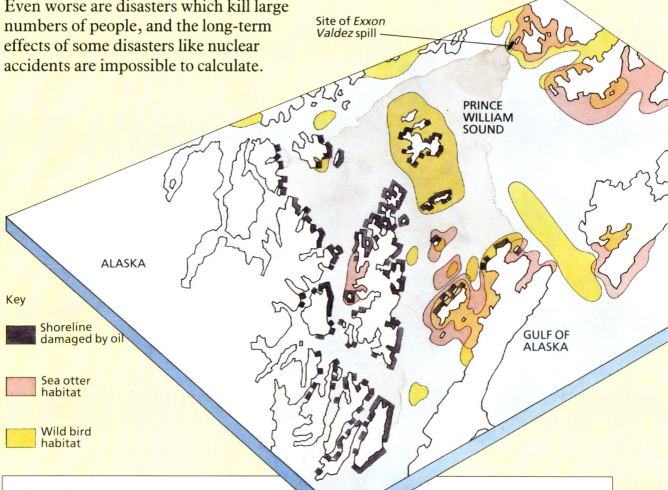

Site of *Exxon Valdez* spill

PRINCE WILLIAM SOUND

ALASKA

GULF OF ALASKA

Key

- Shoreline damaged by oil
- Sea otter habitat
- Wild bird habitat

Bhopal 1984

An explosion at a poorly-maintained and badly-managed US-owned pesticide factory in India released a poisonous cloud over slums housing 200,000 people. Well over 2,000 people died and many thousands more were injured or disabled with damaged lungs and eyes.

Bhopal

INDIA

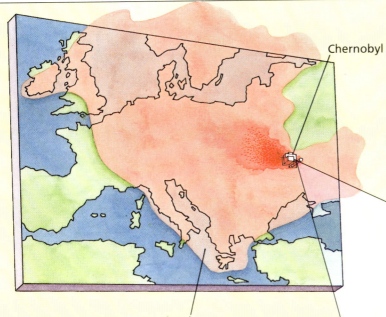

Chernobyl

Radioactive cloud

Chernobyl 1986

A huge explosion at this Soviet nuclear power station caused radioactive material to escape. It spread over Central and Western Europe and Scandinavia, affecting crops and animals. Over 30 people were killed immediately and 200 became very ill. No one knows how many people will die of cancer in the future.

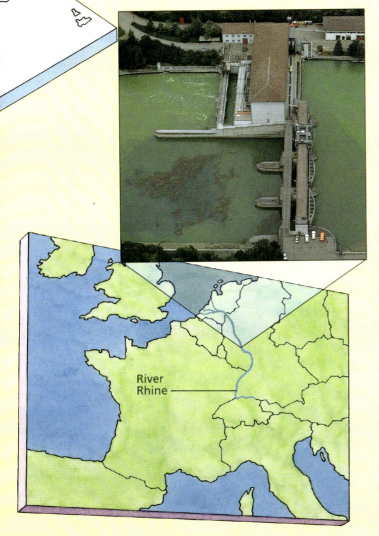

River Rhine

River Rhine

The largest and dirtiest river in Western Europe, the Rhine, supplies drinking water to 20 million people. It carries polluted waste from the large chemical factories along its banks to the North Sea. During a factory fire in 1986, 30 tons of toxic chemicals were washed into the river, killing almost everything for 62-124 miles of its length.

CHAPTER FOUR

CONTROLLING POLLUTION

Pollution and its effects are increasing, mainly due to the ever-growing population. It has left no corner of the world untouched. What can we do to rescue our environment and ourselves? At home we can be less wasteful with energy, reuse or recycle as much of our trash as possible, use unleaded gasoline and limit our use of cars. But to be really effective worldwide we must persuade governments to control or ban pollution from power stations, industry and vehicles. Our goal must be a sustainable lifestyle, using renewable resources and finding uses for waste products instead of creating pollution by discarding them.

Saving energy

By simply using less electricity we can cut down on the release of several pollutants. Power stations are one of the major producers of carbon dioxide, sulfur dioxide and nitrogen oxides, thus they contribute greatly to the increasing greenhouse effect and acid rain. Industry is a large user of electricity and huge savings could be made there with the right inducements. At home we can save electricity in many ways. Over one half of all domestic energy is used for heating and cooking. One of the best ways of saving energy is to increase the insulation of our homes, minimizing the heat loss, and by installing and adjusting temperature controls so that we only have heat when and where it is needed. Many household electrical appliances could be more efficient, doing the same job with less electricity. For example, ordinary refrigerators use about four kilowatt hours of electricity per day, but the most efficient use about half this, and new ones are being developed which will run on only one kWh per day. More efficient light bulbs have also been developed. These reductions in electricity output also save the consumer money, so

△ Wind turbines, like these in Belgium, can provide pollution-free electricity.

◁ Bicycles are a cheap, efficient and clean form of transportation.

next time you buy an electrical appliance ask yourself if you really need it and if it is energy efficient.

About one third of the 2.8 billion tons of oil used worldwide each year is burned as gasoline and diesel by cars and trucks, which are not very fuel efficient. We could increase their fuel efficiency by traveling more slowly (though this would probably need law enforcement), by keeping the engine well-maintained, and by designing cars for fuel economy. An increase in efficiency of 20 percent would save about 200 million tons of oil every year. The oil crisis of the 1970s (when the price of oil rose dramatically) made manufacturers first consider fuel efficiency, and great improvements have been made. However, it would be even better to use public transportation more and private cars less. An average family car can carry four people six miles using 0.2 gallons of fuel, while a bus can carry 40 people six miles with one gallon of fuel, using 2.5 times less fuel per person. Wider use of public transportation would also mean fewer cars would be made, reducing the energy used and the pollution caused by the car manufacturing industry.

Alternative energy sources

We could further reduce pollution created by burning fossil fuels if we produced more of our electricity from renewable sources, which are also environmentally-friendly. Since the fossil fuel supply will not last forever we will have to find other ways to make electricity. At the moment, fossil fuels provide 62 percent of the world's electricity, 19 percent comes from hydroelectricity, 17 percent from nuclear power and only two percent from other sources. Hydroelectricity is already used wherever there are suitable rivers and dams to supply the power, but solar, wind, wave, tidal, geothermal and burning waste and biofuels are only just beginning to be exploited. On a global scale these renewable energy sources could theoretically provide all our present electricity requirements, but much more research, work and commitment are needed to develop the technology necessary to extract usable energy.

Already large wind farms in the United States use arrays of wind turbines with blades up to 98 yards across to produce electricity, and similar systems are being tested elsewhere. France has a tidal generator, and wave systems are being investigated, as well as geothermal sources which use heat from below the earth's surface to provide steam to run an electric generator. These are already in use in New Zealand and Iceland. Solar power, though most efficient in sunny climates like the southwestern United States, has potential for providing power or heating in most countries. Solar cells convert sunlight directly into electricity, while solar panels use the Sun's energy to heat water, providing domestic heating or hot water. So far all these methods have been attempted only on a small scale and have proved more expensive than traditional electricity sources, but this will change as the fossil fuels begin to run out and their rarity makes them increasingly expensive to extract.

Another source of electricity, which could solve two problems at once, would be to burn the methane gas released by garbage dumps, or the contents of the dumps themselves, to provide heat for power generation. This would remove the pollution problems methane gas causes (as a greenhouse gas) as well as providing a method of permanently disposing of waste, though there would have to be careful controls to prevent further pollutants escaping as gas to harm the environment or human health.

△ Sunlight is concentrated for heat.

Stopping pollution from escaping

There are two ways to tackle industrial pollution, either to make less pollution in the first place, or to stop the pollution from escaping into the environment. It is already possible to remove 90 percent of the sulfur dioxide from the gases that escape up the chimneys of coal- and oil-burning power stations.

There are several methods, and the best ones convert the sulfur dioxide pollutant into a useful product. Most commonly it is bubbled through a limestone slurry, producing gypsum which is used in the construction industry to make plasterboard and cement.

There are many options, if we can persuade industry to use them. All of them will make electricity a little more expensive; by about 10 percent for cleaning flue gases. In the rich industrialized countries this is not much to pay for a cleaner environment, but poorer developing nations may need help to prevent industrial pollution from increasing in their countries.

We can also clean up the pollution from cars. Most cars are now adapted to use lead-

Cleaning up the River Thames
In spite of sewage works along its banks, the River Thames, in England, was so polluted in the 1950s that no fish could survive there. Cleaning up started in 1953 with improvements to sewage works and controls on pollution from industry. Now about 100 different kinds of fish live in the Thames.

△ Newspapers are collected for recycling.

free gasoline, which completely eliminates poisonous lead from exhaust gases. In the United States many places have already banned leaded gasoline and the use of lead-free gasoline is being actively encouraged in Europe. Catalytic converters can only be used with lead-free gasoline. When these are fitted to the exhaust pipes of cars they greatly reduce the amounts of carbon monoxide, nitrogen oxides and unburned hydrocarbons emitted by making the gases react together, though carbon dioxide is still released. In 1975 the United States introduced laws to encourage the increased use of catalytic converters, and they can be fitted to cars relatively easily. An alternative approach for the future is an improved kind of engine now being developed; the "lean burn" engine. This would burn fuel so efficiently that it would produce much less polluting gas, but unfortunately would still release the nitrogen oxides that contribute to acid rain.

These are only some examples of ways we can reduce the pollution escaping into the environment. Other ways include designing new industrial plants so that they produce less pollution in the first place, or finding uses for unwanted by-products instead of discarding them all as waste. In the long term these approaches will probably be cheaper and more effective than treating waste gases, solids and liquids to remove pollutants.

We could also find less harmful alternatives to some products which become pollutants, and this has already been done in the case of pesticides. When the dangers of the pesticides DDT and dieldrin were realized, replacements were developed which are much safer to use. Now scientists are looking for alternative gases to use in refrigerators and air-conditioners instead of the CFCs which destroy the ozone layer.

Recycling and reusing rubbish

Since World War II people in the western world have gradually gotten used to living in a "throw away" society. We discard things we no longer want with little thought for their possible use to others or their alternative uses. Most of the things we buy are well-wrapped, usually in several layers of plastic. In the United States more than 432,000 tons of garbage are produced each day, 80 percent of which is carted to landfills. Each individual in America produced three and a half pounds of waste each day. However, recycling programs are being implemented in many areas. Ten states have mandatory recycling. Recycling bottles, metals and paper can slow down the use of limited natural resources, reduce the quantities of garbage to be disposed of, and in many cases, save energy, which in itself reduces pollution. Organic waste, including food waste and vegetable matter, can be recycled by turning it into compost and using it on the land instead of artificial fertilizers. Many people collect newspapers and cans, and return glass bottles to recycling centers, but after that it is up to industry to use them. Recycling saves

△ Some factories make new paper from waste paper instead of from trees.

considerable energy – every ton of glass recycled saves 20 gallons of oil, and resmelting aluminum cans makes energy savings of 95 percent.

Plastics are more of a problem. They come in many different forms and cannot easily be recycled. If they are, the end product has limited uses because it is a mixture of many different types of plastic. The best course of action is to avoid plastic as much as possible. Use your own shopping bags at the supermarket instead of the throw-away plastic ones which will last for thousands of years on the garbage dump.

Industry also recycles some of its waste products, though this practice needs to be emphasized. Many factories, particularly in the metal industries, make use of both new and recycled materials, and in addition, waste from one factory can sometimes be useful to another. Two neighboring factories in the United States were able to take advantage of this. One was throwing away alkaline sludge from its water-softening plant, while the other was buying an alkali to treat its acidic waste water. Now the waste from one is being used to treat the other's waste product, saving money and decreasing pollution. This is by no means the only example, and will become a greater consideration for industry in the future when our dwindling supplies of raw materials become more expensive, as does the cost of dumping garbage. In the end, the garbage dumps of today, which contain many useful materials, may well be mined to extract raw materials for the future.

Organic farming – food for the future?
With the world population growing fast and likely to keep on growing for some time, farmers have had to produce more and more food by improving their efficiency. The Green Revolution has helped them to do this. Scientists have bred new strains of crops that produce more food per plant, and have provided the farmer with artificial fertilizers to help increase yield, and pesticides to minimize pest damage. This has enabled food production to increase massively between 1950 and 1980, in fact more rapidly than the population.

Theoretically there is no need for anyone to go hungry if food is distributed evenly. This increase in food production is a great achievement, but the fertilizers and pesticides, necessary in preventing famine around the world, also cause pollution when they wash out of the soil and into the water supply. Intensive farming has also caused other problems, including soil erosion, since artificial fertilizers do not enrich the soil in the same way as compost and manure, and it can be blown away if there are no hedges and trees for windbreaks.

Some people advocate a return to the more traditional methods of organic farming, but this might not produce enough food to keep up with the population worldwide. In organic farming animal manure is used as fertilizer, and crops are rotated, with part of the land allowed to lie fallow to recover from crop production. Pest damage is also reduced by crop rotation and mixed farming. This kind of farming undoubtedly causes less pollution and is increasingly popular in the western world where there is no shortage of food and people are more aware of the possible dangers of pesticides in their food. However, organic farms produce 10 to 20 percent less food per acre. In the last five years world food production has not grown as fast as the population, and reducing it further by changing to organic farming methods could be disastrous.

Perhaps the answer lies in compromise. Technology can provide us with improved crops that are more resistant to pests and disease and have higher yields. There are other methods of reducing pest damage, for example by encouraging natural predators so there would be less need for pesticides. Changes in farming practice to stop soil erosion and using natural fertilizers wherever possible would reduce the need for artificial fertilizers. Also a change in diet would help. In the richer countries, not

△ Organic farming reduces pollution.

only do many people eat too much for their health, but their diets contain too high a proportion of meat. Meat is expensive to produce because animals are not very efficient at turning their food into meat. A healthier diet with less meat would leave more food for others because less grain would be needed for animal feed.

Pollution and politics
We can all help to reduce pollution, but many of the effects are international, or even worldwide, and these can only be tackled by governments working together. Organizations like Greenpeace and Friends of the Earth have been working for many years to open our eyes to the damage pollution does to the planet, and to pressurize governments into doing something about it. Their campaigns have gradually become more successful, especially over the last 10 years, and the

△ "Green" parties campaign to preserve the earth from human misuse.

"green movement" has gathered popular support in many countries. This is what is needed to persuade governments to act, because many of the measures to control pollution are expensive and will have to be enforced by laws. The cost of cleaning up the environment will have to be paid for by all of us, either directly or by government subsidies, which our taxes pay for. Already some measures are supported by subsidies; lead-free gasoline is cheaper in many countries. We will probably need massive subsidies to persuade us to use public transportation more than our cars, and industrial costs of pollution control may be passed on to us in more expensive industrial products.

Already there are a multitude of national laws and international agreements regulating pollution, including the atmospheric testing of nuclear bombs, dumping of waste at sea, gas emissions from car exhausts and factory chimneys, the production of CFCs, and so on. Some of these are difficult to enforce, like dumping at sea, while others only operate in a few countries. Many countries need a lot of

pushing to sign an agreement that would cost industries money. The countries most affected by acid rain have difficulty trying to overcome the reluctance of the acid rain-exporting countries to sign an agreement controlling sulfur dioxide emissions. Similarly, the worst producers of carbon dioxide require more evidence of the greenhouse effect before they will agree to reduce emissions. Few politicians look further than the next elections, and pollution measures started now may not show results for many years to come.

The industrialized countries have caused most of our pollution problems, and the developing world has been on the receiving end so far. However, these nations are now trying to improve their living standards which will mean more industries and greater use of energy and transportation, leading to even more pollution if not controlled. These poorer countries will not be able to afford the expensive equipment needed to limit pollution without help from the developed world. Only by working together can we keep this planet a safe and pleasant place to live.

GLOSSARY

acid rain natural rain made more acidic by air pollution from cars and power stations. It damages plants, forests, rivers and lakes.

acre a measure of land area. There are 640 acres in one square mile.

bioconcentration the build up of pollutants stored in the body as larger creatures eat smaller ones, reaching poisonous levels.

CFCs (chlorofluorocarbons) stable, nontoxic gases used in refrigerators and spray cans which damage the ozone layer.

developing countries poorer countries with little industry and mainly rural economies.

dioxins extremely poisonous pollutants that occur when pesticides are manufactured and when plastics are not burned properly.

effluent any waste water or liquids from homes and factories.

fertilizer natural or artificial plant food added to the soil to increase plant growth.

global warming slow warming of the earth due to the increase of polluting gases which insulate the planet.

greenhouse effect traps the heat from the Sun keeping the earth warm. "Greenhouse gases" include carbon dioxide, methane, nitrous oxide and CFCs.

heavy metals include the metals mercury, lead and cadmium. They cannot be destroyed and can build up in the environment and in the body. Some are extremely poisonous.

industrialized countries rich countries where industry provides more jobs than agriculture.

nitrates natural substances found in fertilizers, essential for plant growth.

nutrients foodstuffs needed for growth and for sustaining plant and animal life.

organic farming farming without artificial fertilizers or pesticides. Organic materials contain carbon and hydrogen and are the basis of all living things.

ozone layer a region in the atmosphere about 19 miles high that contains a very small amount of ozone gas, which absorbs the Sun's harmful ultraviolet rays.

PCBs (polychlorinated biphenyls) toxic materials used in electrical goods, now banned in Europe except in sealed units. They can only be destroyed by burning.

pesticides chemicals used to kill insects and diseases that attack plants, and also weeds that interfere with crop growth.

phosphates substances in fertilizers which are essential for plant growth. They are also used in detergents. Excessive quantities can cause serious pollution.

photosynthesis method by which green plants use the energy in sunlight to grow, using up carbon dioxide and releasing oxygen.

PVC (polyvinyl chloride) a plastic with many uses. Bags and bottles can be made out of it.

radioactivity production of radiation as some atoms in a material break down into other atoms. The "radiation" is rays and tiny particles which harm living things.

recycling reusing unwanted materials and goods instead of throwing them away.

reprocessing chemical treatment of used nuclear power station fuel rods to recover any useful plutonium and uranium fuels.

toxic poisonous to animals or plants.

INDEX

Photographic Credits:
Cover: Spectrum Colour Library; intro page and pages 18-19 and 28-29: Robert Harding Library; pages 4-5 and 31: Eye Ubiquitous; pages 5, 10 and 24: Topham Picture Library; pages 6, 8, 29 and 32: J. Allan Cash Library; page 7 top: Associated Press 7 bottom: NASA; pages 9 and 25: Ajax News and Features Library; pages 11, 12, 17 and 21: Hutchison Library; page 13: Food and Agriculture Organizations; page 22: Popperfoto; page 22-23: Magnum Photos; pages 25 and 27 left: Frank Spooner Agency; page 30: SERI; page 33: US Department of Agriculture.

PRINTED IN BELGIUM BY
proost
INTERNATIONAL BOOK PRODUCTION